BASKETBALL
How It Works

Sports Illustrated KIDS

BY SUZANNE SLADE

Consultant:
John Fontanella
Department of Physics
U.S. Naval Academy

CAPSTONE PRESS
a capstone imprint

Sports Illustrated KIDS The Science of Sports is published by Capstone Press,
1710 Roe Crest Drive, North Mankato, Minnesota 56003.
www.capstonepub.com

102013
007833R

Library of Congress Cataloging-in-Publication Data
Slade, Suzanne.
    Basketball : how it works / by Suzanne Slade.
    p. cm. — (Sports Illustrated KIDS. The science of sports)
    Includes bibliographical references and index.
    Summary: "Describes the science behind the sport of basketball, including offense, defense, arenas,
and trick plays" — Provided by publisher.
    ISBN 978-1-4296-4021-3 (library binding)
    ISBN 978-1-4296-4873-8 (paperback)
    ISBN 978-1-4765-0186-4 (e-book)
    1. Basketball — Juvenile literature. 2. Sports sciences — Juvenile literature. I. Title. II. Series.
GV885.1.S52 2010
796.323 — dc22
                                                                            2009028508

Editorial Credits
Anthony Wacholtz, editor; Ted Williams, designer; Jo Miller, media researcher;
    Eric Manske, production specialist

Many of the statistics in this book came from John Fontanella's *The Physics of Basketball*.

Design Elements
Shutterstock/Eray Haciosmanoglu; fantasista; kamphi; Makarov Vladyslav; mark cinotti; Steve Cukrov

Photo Credits
AP Images/Tom Pidgeon, 22
Capstone Press/Farhana Hossain, 27 (bottom)
NBAE via Getty Images Inc./Bill Baptist, 31; Nathaniel S. Butler, 27 (top); Ray Amati, 45
Shutterstock/David Lee, 39 (wood); hkannn, 37; Jut, 27 (basketball); Lonesome_tiger, 39 (concrete);
    Thomas Fredriksen, 39 (asphalt)
Sports Illustrated/Al Tielemans, 42; Bill Frakes, 13, 17, 28; Bob Rosato, 1, 4, 8, 10, 15, 20, 23;
    Damian Strohmeyer, 6, 11, 32, 43; David E. Klutho, 21, 24, 29; Jeffery A. Salter, 35;
    John Biever, cover (bottom right), 3, 26, 40, 41; John W. McDonough, cover (top),
    cover (bottom left), cover (bottom middle), 9, 12, 14, 18, 25, 30, 33, 34, 36, 38; Simon Bruty, 44

TABLE OF CONTENTS

▷ B-BALL AND SCIENCE

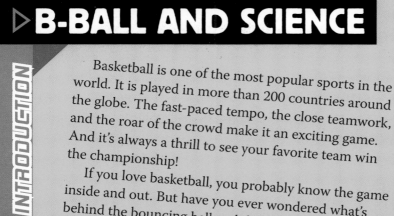

Basketball is one of the most popular sports in the world. It is played in more than 200 countries around the globe. The fast-paced tempo, the close teamwork, and the roar of the crowd make it an exciting game. And it's always a thrill to see your favorite team win the championship!

If you love basketball, you probably know the game inside and out. But have you ever wondered what's behind the bouncing ball and the three-point basket? Basketball, like all sports, can be explained by science.

momentum
The player gains momentum when he begins to move toward the basket for a rebound.

James Naismith, a physical education teacher in Springfield, Massachusetts, invented the game of basketball in 1891.

force
The player uses force to push the ball toward the basket.

friction
The player uses friction to begin moving along the floor.

gravity
The player fights gravity to take a jump shot.

Good offense requires players to dribble, pass, and shoot the ball with great skill. They combine these skills with well-rehearsed plays to move the ball down the court and score.

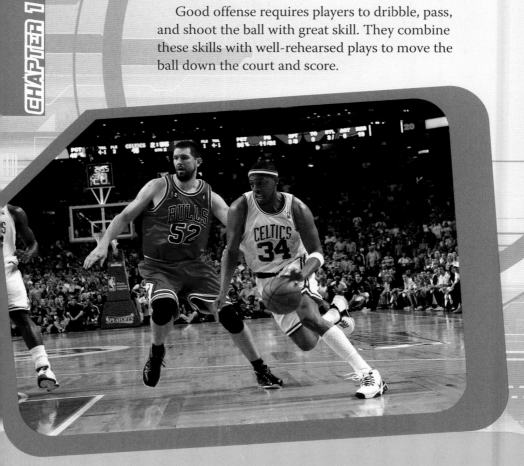

BASKETBALL BOUNCINESS

Along with the skill of players, the basketball affects the success of an offense. The bounciness of a basketball is so important to the game that it is checked by the International Basketball Federation (IBF). The IBF requires that the ball bounces between 1.2 meters (3.9 feet) and 1.4 meters (4.6 feet), measured from the top of the ball. The ball must reach this height when dropped from 1.8 meters (5.9 feet), measured from the bottom of the ball. The air pressure inside a ball is measured in pounds per square inch (psi). The bounce is mostly determined by the pressure.

	Men's Basketball (size 7)	Women's Basketball (size 6)
Diameter	9.4 in.	9.1 in.
Weight	20–22 oz.	18–20 oz.
Recommended Air Pressure	7–9 psi	7–9 psi

If a ball is inflated to 8 psi, a force of 23 pounds pushes out on each square inch of the inside surface of the ball. The 23 pounds of force is a combination of the 8 psi and the atmospheric pressure, which is about 15 psi.

WHY A BASKETBALL BOUNCES

A basketball is filled with air made of tiny **MOLECULES**. Air molecules are always moving and bumping into one another. When a basketball hits the floor, the part of the ball that hits the floor is pushed in. The air molecules are pushed together and begin to move faster. The molecules slam into the inside surface of the ball, and the outside surface pushes against the floor. The floor then pushes up on the ball, causing the bounce.

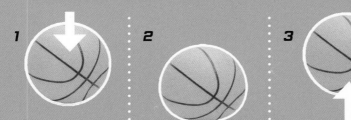

1   2   3

A warm basketball is bouncier than a cold basketball. This is partly because molecules move faster at higher temperatures. The molecules in the warm ball hit the inside surface of the ball at a higher speed. The ball's surface then pushes on the ground with more force than the surface of a cold ball.

MOLECULE — the atoms that make up the smallest unit of a substance

7

KEEP DRIBBLING!

When a player stops dribbling but his feet keep moving forward, he will hear the referee's whistle. Traveling violation! To avoid traveling, a player must be able to quickly stop his **MOMENTUM**.

momentum = mass x velocity

A player uses many muscles, such as leg, back, and abdominal muscles, to stop moving and avoid traveling.

mass

The stopping motion created by the muscle groups moves through the body to the feet. Friction between the player's feet and the floor creates a force. This force opposes the momentum and allows the player to stop.

velocity

momentum

MOMENTUM — a property of a moving object equal to its mass times its velocity

VELOCITY — a measurement of both the speed and direction an object is moving

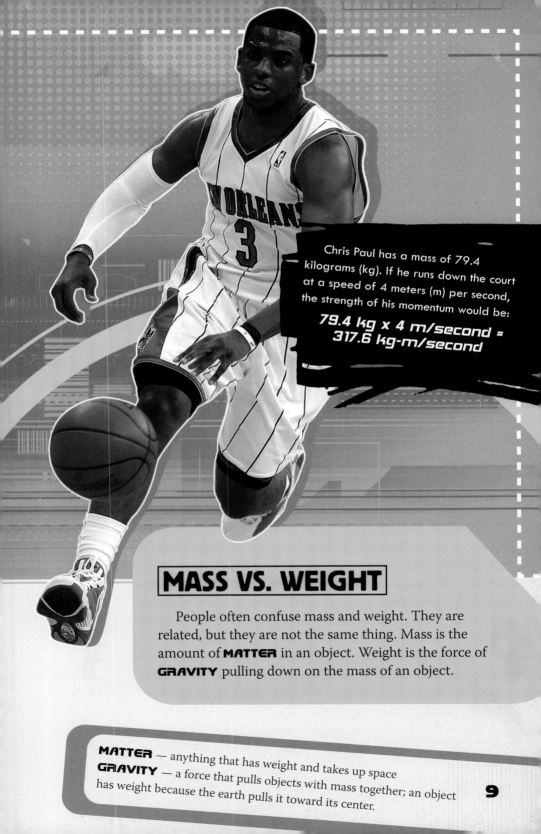

Chris Paul has a mass of 79.4 kilograms (kg). If he runs down the court at a speed of 4 meters (m) per second, the strength of his momentum would be:

79.4 kg x 4 m/second = 317.6 kg-m/second

MASS VS. WEIGHT

People often confuse mass and weight. They are related, but they are not the same thing. Mass is the amount of **MATTER** in an object. Weight is the force of **GRAVITY** pulling down on the mass of an object.

MATTER — anything that has weight and takes up space
GRAVITY — a force that pulls objects with mass together; an object has weight because the earth pulls it toward its center.

SHOOT AND SCORE!

Accurate shooting is the most important offensive skill. Good shooters will use a wrist snap during their shots. A wrist snap uses static friction to put backspin on the ball. Backspin creates ball lift and makes it less likely that the ball will bounce off the rim.

normal force

static friction force

During a wrist snap, a player's hand puts two forces on the ball. The normal force is upward and perpendicular to the shooting hand. The second force, the static friction force, occurs with a flick of the wrist. The fingers move with the surface of the ball, causing it to spin and accelerate. These two forces go against gravity and give the ball its velocity.

A wrist snap happens in one-tenth of a second.

The ball rotates about 1/8 of a revolution while in contact with the hand.

The static friction force occurs when there is no slipping between the surface of the ball and the player's hand.

Backspin also lifts the ball during flight.

A correct wrist snap creates a backspin of two **REVOLUTIONS** per second. Backspin helps a ball move smoothly through the surrounding air molecules.

When a player shoots, he must push the ball with enough upward force to overcome the pull of gravity.

REVOLUTION — when an object spins 360 degrees and ends in its original position

11

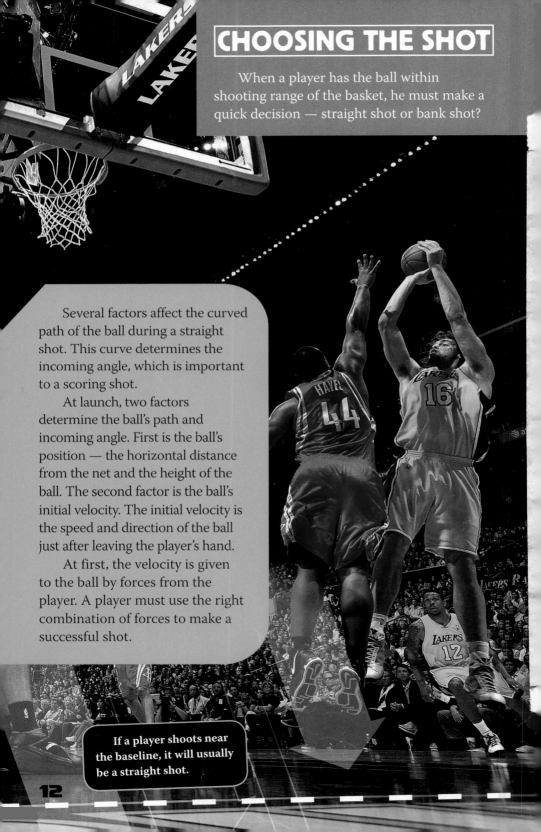

CHOOSING THE SHOT

When a player has the ball within shooting range of the basket, he must make a quick decision — straight shot or bank shot?

Several factors affect the curved path of the ball during a straight shot. This curve determines the incoming angle, which is important to a scoring shot.

At launch, two factors determine the ball's path and incoming angle. First is the ball's position — the horizontal distance from the net and the height of the ball. The second factor is the ball's initial velocity. The initial velocity is the speed and direction of the ball just after leaving the player's hand.

At first, the velocity is given to the ball by forces from the player. A player must use the right combination of forces to make a successful shot.

If a player shoots near the baseline, it will usually be a straight shot.

incoming angle

Putting a round ball through a larger round hoop should be an easy fit, right? That's true if a basketball falls straight down directly over the rim. But that rarely happens. A basketball usually comes toward the rim at an angle. The incoming angle of the ball "changes" the shape of the rim opening that the basketball passes through.

Imagine a ball thrown straight at the rim with an incoming angle of 0 degrees. From the point of view of the ball, the round rim would look like a straight line. The ball could not pass through the hoop at this angle. In men's basketball, a player must shoot the ball using an incoming angle greater than 33.3 degrees. If the angle is less than 33.3 degrees, the ball won't fit through the basket. For women's basketball, the incoming angle must be greater than 32.1 degrees because the ball is .3 inch (.8 centimeter) smaller.

SCIENCE OF THE BANK

During a bank shot, the way the ball comes off the backboard and through the hoop is determined by three things:

1) where the ball hits the backboard
2) the velocity of the ball when it hits the backboard
3) the spin of the ball as it hits the backboard

HITTING THE TREY

Fans go crazy when their team scores a three-point basket. A player shoots from behind a curved line to make a three-pointer. In front of the basket, the line is 21 feet (6.4 meters) from the hoop. The ball must be thrown with the proper force to travel this distance. Players use science — three different kinds of levers — to create enough force to sink a three-pointer.

A lever is one type of a simple machine. Scientists define a simple machine as a machine that does work with one movement. A lever is simply a bar that moves around a fixed point called a fulcrum. When an effort force is applied to the lever, the lever feels a resistance force and counteracts it.

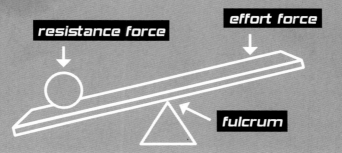

resistance force

effort force

fulcrum

There are three classes of levers: first, second, and third. The position of the fulcrum, effort force, and resistance force on the lever determines the class. During a three-point shot, a basketball player uses all three types of levers.

A first-class lever has a fulcrum located between the effort and resistance forces. Strong neck muscles create the effort force. The effort force allows the lever to counteract the resistance force and support the weight of the head. The fulcrum is the joint where the skull connects to the spine.

For a third-class lever, the effort force is between the resistance force and fulcrum. When shooting the ball, the elbow is the fulcrum. The effort force comes from the arm muscles. It allows the lever to counteract the resistance force and push the weight of the ball.

The resistance force is between the effort force and fulcrum in a second-class lever. When a player pushes up on his toes, the largest toe joint acts as the fulcrum. Calf muscles provide the effort force. The effort force allows the lever to counteract the resistance force and lift the weight of the body.

FREE THROW FORM

Fouled players are often awarded free throws. The player stands 15 feet (4.6 meters) from the basket at the free throw line. He must shoot the ball with the correct velocity to score the extra point. Proper spin also helps.

Pro basketball players practice thousands of free throws every season. Players often repeat the same sets of arm and leg movements with every practice shot. They develop habits so they can repeat the right moves to score free throws.

The arc, or height, of a throw depends on the upward force the player puts on the ball. More upward force results in a higher arc. Too low of an arc can lead to a reduced hoop opening that may be too small for the ball to go through.

Many players put backspin on the ball to help it drop in the basket if it lands on the rim. A spinning ball creates friction when it contacts the rim. The friction slows down the ball, increasing the chance that it will go into the basket.

distance from rim
15 feet (4.6 meters)

backspin

height of rim
10 feet (3 meters) from ground

WILT "THE STILT" CHAMBERLAIN

It's a well-known fact that NBA basketball legend Wilt Chamberlain wasn't the best free throw shooter. His career average was a terrible 51 percent. But in his high school years, Chamberlain's free throw tosses had a higher arc. At that time, his shooting percentage was quite good — 80 percent. As he got older, Chamberlain couldn't bend his injured knees as easily. He believed this loss of motion changed his arc, which hurt his ability to make free throws.

Chamberlain had one unbelievable night of free throw shooting in 1962. He made a record-breaking 28 free throws out of 32 attempts against the New York Knicks. Wilt also scored a record 100 points during the game.

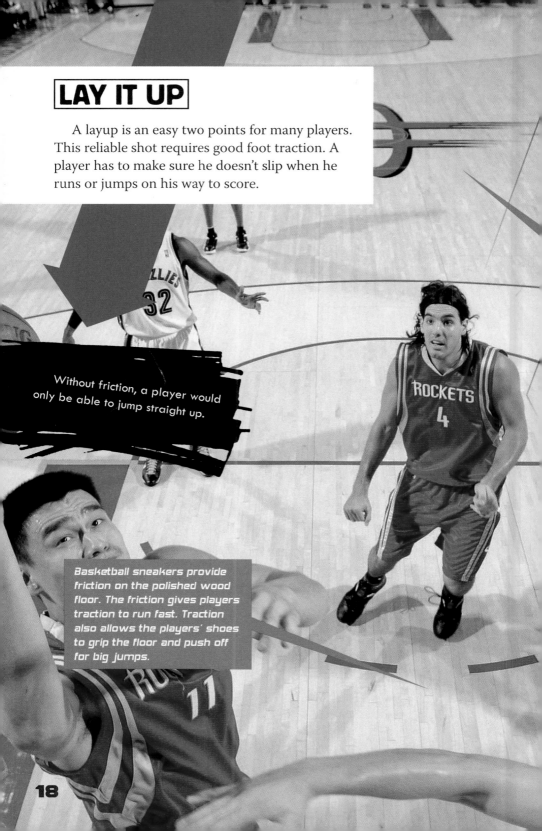

LAY IT UP

A layup is an easy two points for many players. This reliable shot requires good foot traction. A player has to make sure he doesn't slip when he runs or jumps on his way to score.

Without friction, a player would only be able to jump straight up.

Basketball sneakers provide friction on the polished wood floor. The friction gives players traction to run fast. Traction also allows the players' shoes to grip the floor and push off for big jumps.

GET A GRIP

Long ago, shoes were made of leather and cloth. These slick materials did not create enough friction. People wearing them often slipped while walking. In the early 1900s, shoe manufacturers solved this problem by putting rubber soles on the bottom of shoes. They named these new shoes sneakers. The rubber increased friction between the shoe and the surface below it. This meant a safer, non-slip shoe for basketball and much more!

Friction and the normal force between the player's hand and the ball are important during a layup. They overcome gravity to allow the player to direct the ball to the right spot on the backboard.

SLAM DUNK!

Fans love to see their team make a basket, but one shot is a real crowd pleaser — the slam dunk. Basketball players fight against gravity when they are in contact with the floor. How high a player jumps depends on the amount of force created by the player's leg muscles while he is in contact with the floor.

Gravity causes free-falling objects to accelerate toward earth at a rate of 32.2 feet (9.8 meters) per second squared (shown as 32.2 feet/s^2). For each second an object falls, its speed will increase at a rate of 32.2 feet per second.

Don't blink! Most slam dunks last less than .9 second.

A player bends his knees to push away from the floor. Bending the knees a small amount allows the muscles to generate only a small force and therefore a short jump height. Bending the knees too much can cause a loss of balance. Through practice, players learn how much to bend their knees to get the highest jumps while keeping their balance.

Swinging your arms up before your feet leave the court adds height to your jump. When your arms move upward, your body is pushed down. This downward force increases the force the legs use to push off.

Why do basketball players seems to hang in the air at the top of a dunk? This illusion is the result of gravity. A player's upward speed decreases in the first half of the jump. It continues to decrease until it reaches zero at the top of the jump. As the player returns to the ground, his downward speed increases as he gets closer to the ground. Because most of the time is spent in the upper half of the jump, the player looks like he is floating.

The hang time of a 3-foot (.9-meter) jump is .87 second.

About 70 percent of the jump time is spent in the top half of the jump.

Because of gravity, the player's speed increases as his height decreases.

Because of gravity, the player's speed decreases as his height increases.

3 feet

1.5 feet

About 30 percent of the jump time is spent in the bottom half of the jump.

SHATTER THE BOARDS

A slam dunk is an incredible feat to watch, but a player must be careful not to grab hold of the rim. The results can be shattering!

Backboards are made of a material called tempered glass. Tempered glass is four to five times stronger than regular glass. Tempered glass is heated above a certain temperature, known as the glass transition temperature. After heating, the surface of the sheet of glass is cooled quickly. This process tempers the glass, creating a surface that is more resistant to hits. But the inside of the glass is easily broken.

It takes less than one second for an entire backboard to shatter.

A backboard is more likely to break if the player grabs onto the rim and lifts himself up. The extra force on the rim may cause the rim to snap off the backboard or shatter the glass.

The backboard can break when a player grabs an improperly mounted rim during a slam dunk. The metal end of the rim pushes inward. Tension is created at the edge of the glass, and a small crack forms. This crack travels quickly through the glass. Hundreds of new cracks form, and the board shatters!

THROUGH THE ZONE

Offensive players have to work together to get around a zone defense. Each defensive player stays in a certain area of the court to protect the basket. Players on offense often use bounce passes to move the ball past a zone defense for an inside shot.

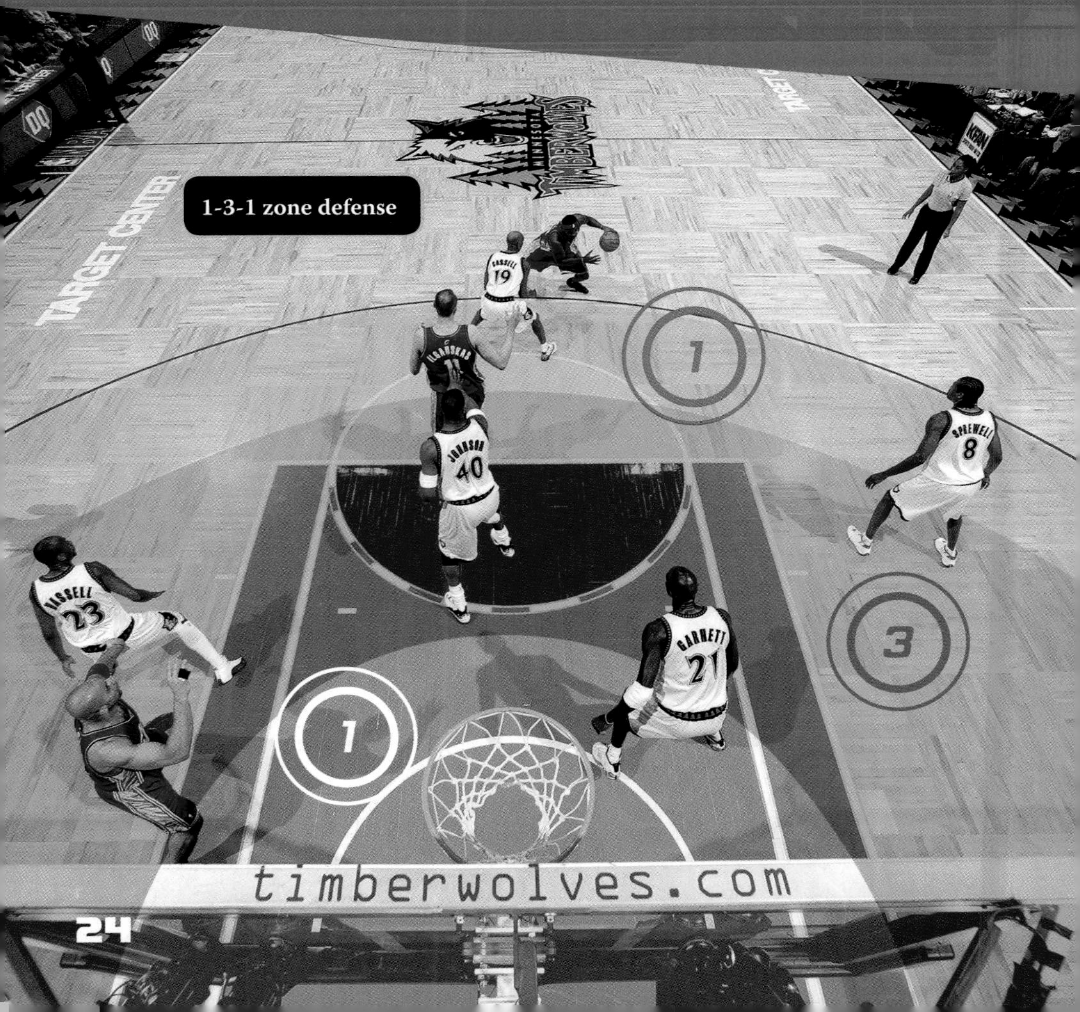

1-3-1 zone defense

timberwolves.com

The angle at which the ball hits the ground during a bounce pass is about the same as its rebound angle. Experienced players can easily predict the path of a bounce pass unless the ball is thrown with spin.

The bounce pass

Friction between the player's hand and the ball allows the player to put spin on the ball during a bounce pass.

topspin

A bounce pass with topspin moves faster after hitting the floor than a ball with no spin. The forward spin lowers the friction between the ball and the floor.

backspin

A ball with backspin moves slower after hitting the floor than a ball thrown with no spin. Backspin increases the friction between the ball and the floor.

left spin

A bounce pass thrown with left spin will veer left after it hits the floor. Players often use it to move the ball around an opponent.

right spin

Players also use a right-spin bounce pass to fool opponents. A right spin causes the ball to veer right after hitting the floor.

CHAPTER 2

▷ DEFENSE

A strong defense works together like a well-oiled machine. The goals are to stop the other team from scoring and to regain control of the ball.

ON GUARD

In a man-to-man defense, each defensive player is assigned to a player on offense. The defensive player tries to predict the moves of his opponent. He has to react quickly to stop the other team from scoring. Defensive players respond to the moves of their opponents. They can jump up to block a shot or reach out to steal a pass.

In the heat of a game, a player watches the ball constantly. But he also watches his opponents out of the corners of his eyes.

A player's eyes can track movements up to 30 feet (9 meters) per second. A player moving at that speed could run the entire length of a basketball court in three seconds!

A player's reaction time is about .25 seconds. This is the amount of time it takes a player to move, or react, to an action of his opponent.

EYES WIDE OPEN

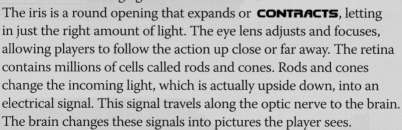

iris

cornea

lens

retina

A transparent film called the cornea covers the front of the eye. The cornea focuses the incoming light. The iris is a round opening that expands or **CONTRACTS**, letting in just the right amount of light. The eye lens adjusts and focuses, allowing players to follow the action up close or far away. The retina contains millions of cells called rods and cones. Rods and cones change the incoming light, which is actually upside down, into an electrical signal. This signal travels along the optic nerve to the brain. The brain changes these signals into pictures the player sees.

CONTRACT — to tighten and become smaller

TAKE THE CHARGE

A player dribbles down the court and runs into an opponent, causing the defender to slide across the floor. Referees have to watch carefully to determine if it's a charge, which is an offensive foul, or a block, which is a defensive foul. They often look to see how much the defensive player moved after being hit. That tells them how much momentum was transferred from the running player to the defender.

The total momentum after a charge is the same as before the charge. Any difference would be caused by the effect of the floor on the players during the collision. A moving player also has energy of motion called kinetic energy. The total kinetic energy after a charge is usually a lot smaller than before the charge.

momentum

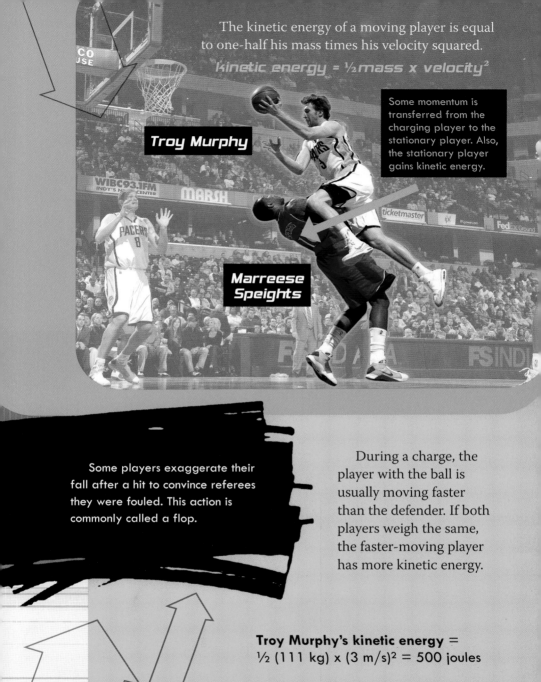

The kinetic energy of a moving player is equal to one-half his mass times his velocity squared.

$$kinetic\ energy = \tfrac{1}{2}\,mass \times velocity^2$$

Some momentum is transferred from the charging player to the stationary player. Also, the stationary player gains kinetic energy.

Troy Murphy

Marreese Speights

Some players exaggerate their fall after a hit to convince referees they were fouled. This action is commonly called a flop.

During a charge, the player with the ball is usually moving faster than the defender. If both players weigh the same, the faster-moving player has more kinetic energy.

Troy Murphy's kinetic energy =
$\tfrac{1}{2}$ (111 kg) x (3 m/s)^2 = 500 joules

Marreese Speights' kinetic energy =
$\tfrac{1}{2}$ (111 kg) x (2 m/s)^2 = 222 joules

GETTING INTO THE GAME

CHAPTER 3

FUELING UP

Basketball players use a lot of energy to run, dribble, jump, and shoot. Their bodies get energy from the food they eat. Players need to fuel up before a game so they are ready for action.

The amount of energy stored in food is measured in calories. A body uses only a few calories while sitting on the bench. But during the game, it burns hundreds more.

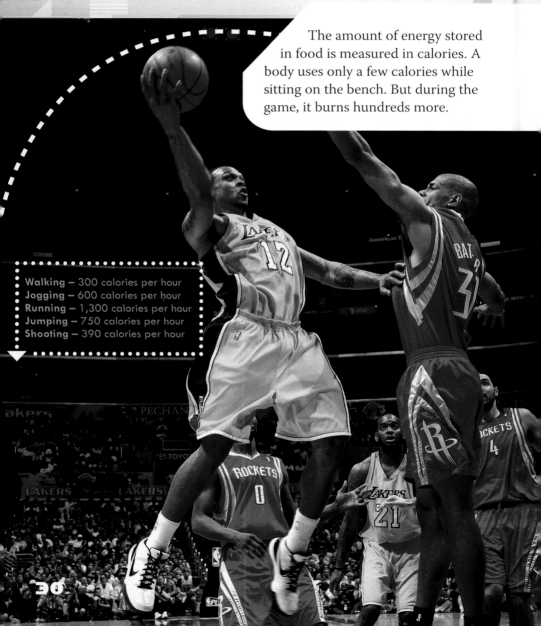

- **Walking** – 300 calories per hour
- **Jogging** – 600 calories per hour
- **Running** – 1,300 calories per hour
- **Jumping** – 750 calories per hour
- **Shooting** – 390 calories per hour

The number of calories burned during an activity depends on the weight of the player. A heavier player will burn more calories than a lighter player while doing the same activity for the same length of time.

EAT UP!

Players fuel up before a big game so they will have plenty of energy. The average NBA player weighs 220 pounds (100 kilograms) and uses about 760 calories during a 48-minute NBA game. These meals add up to 760 calories:

Meal 1	Meal 2
6 oz. roast beef — 330 calories	2 cups spaghetti and sauce — 370 calories
1 cup cooked carrots — 50 calories	1 cup cooked broccoli — 50 calories
baked potato with butter — 130 calories	3 breadsticks — 240 calories
2 rolls — 160 calories	salad and dressing — 100 calories
1 cup milk — 90 calories	glass of water — 0 calories

KEEP MOVING!

A player must be in good physical shape to keep up in a fast-paced basketball game. Every part of the body is involved when a player runs, jumps, blocks, and shoots. The harder the game, the harder a player's body works.

Lungs

As a player moves, the lungs begin to expand and contract faster. More air is pulled into the player's lungs. The oxygen-rich air enters the lungs and passes through the bronchial tubes. Then it enters tiny air sacs called alveoli. The alveoli provide oxygen to the blood vessels.

Heart

When a player runs and jumps, the heart must pump more blood. Blood supplies oxygen for the hard-working muscles. The volume of blood the heart pumps in a minute depends on two things: heart rate and stroke volume. The heart rate is the number of times the heart beats per minute. The stroke volume is how much blood is pumped per heartbeat by each ventricle.

Blood

Blood filled with oxygen is carried away from the lungs by tiny blood vessels called capillaries. The capillaries deliver blood to the pulmonary vein, which connects to the left side of the heart.

Leg muscles

Sometimes leg muscles can burn during a game. This burning sensation is caused by a substance called lactic acid. Lactic acid is created by muscle fibers when they do not get enough oxygen. To get rid of this pain, a player should keep moving. Muscle movement keeps the blood circulating, which helps move the lactic acid away from muscles.

Practice pays off. Regular practice helps players gradually increase the volume of blood their hearts can pump in a minute. A heart that is able to pump more blood provides more oxygen to hard-working muscles.

STRETCHING OUT

Before players hit the court, they prepare their muscles for the game by stretching. Stretching helps avoid muscle tears, strains, and other injuries. It widens a player's range of motion and reduces muscle tension. It also increases energy levels for a quick breakaway down the court.

SKELETAL MUSCLES move the body by contracting and relaxing. Stretching keeps these muscles loose and flexible. The muscles are less likely to tear from overuse. Stretching also protects a player from getting hurt after a sudden force, such as a jump or a hit from another player.

HAMSTRING STRETCH

The hamstring is located on the back of the upper leg. Stretching the hamstrings helps prevent a pulled hamstring. A pulled hamstring can occur during a quick sprint down the court.

▶ BACK STRETCH

Stretching the back improves flexibility and movement. It also helps prevent long-term back injuries.

SKELETAL MUSCLES — muscles that are attached to bones

▶ CALF STRETCH

Healthy calf muscles are needed to run and jump. Stretching prevents calf injuries. For example, stretching can help prevent a strain of the tendon that attaches the calf muscle to the bone.

GROIN STRETCH

A groin stretch prevents groin pulls. During a groin pull, the groin muscle tears away from the inside of the hip.

▶ SHOULDER STRETCH

Stretching shoulder muscles improves range of motion and mobility, allowing the player to move the ball and shoot with more flexibility.

▶ ARM STRETCH

Arm streches improve blood circulation to the shoulders and increase arm range of motion and mobility.

A basketball player uses 12 major leg muscles while running down the court.

ANKLE SPRAINS — OUCH!

The most common basketball injury is a sprained ankle. This painful condition often occurs when a player leaps into the air and lands with a twisted ankle. It can also happen when a player lands on top of another player's foot. Some players wear ankle braces to avoid sprains. An ankle brace absorbs the landing force when a player returns to the ground after a jump.

COOL DOWN

During an action-packed basketball game, a player's body heats up quickly. Perspiration is the body's own cooling method. Perspiration **EVAPORATES** from the skin and changes into a gas. Evaporation happens when the perspiration absorbs energy in the form of heat from the player. Basketball players drink plenty of water and other fluids before, during, and after they play. They need these fluids in order to replenish their cooling system.

The largest organ of the body is the skin. As perspiration evaporates on the surface of the skin, it removes heat from the body.

LEATHER VERSUS PLASTIC

Sweaty hands can make it difficult to handle a basketball. When the NBA introduced a new synthetic ball in June 2006, players soon complained. The plastic surface of the new ball slipped in players' sweaty hands. Players had a hard time handling the ball. After many players complained about the new ball's performance, the NBA brought back the leather-covered balls. The surface of a leather ball absorbs sweat about eight times faster than a synthetic ball.

EVAPORATE — to change from a liquid into a vapor or a gas

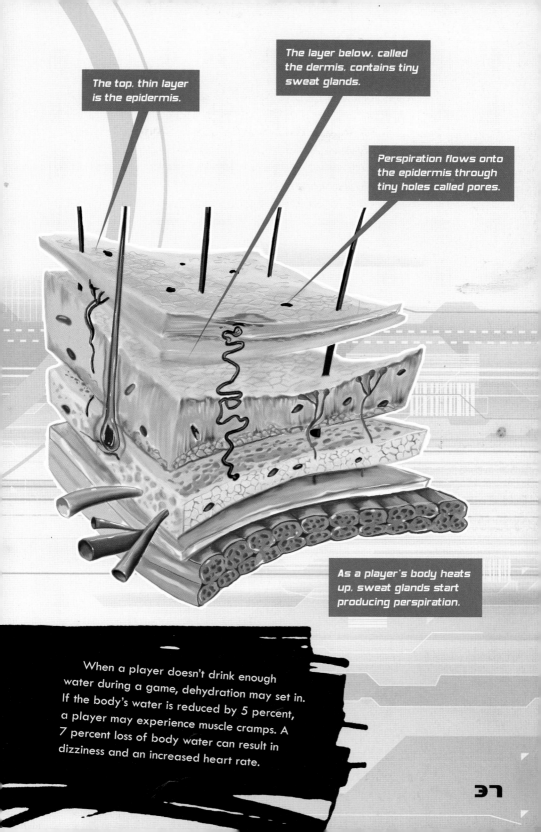

The top, thin layer is the epidermis.

The layer below, called the dermis, contains tiny sweat glands.

Perspiration flows onto the epidermis through tiny holes called pores.

As a player's body heats up, sweat glands start producing perspiration.

When a player doesn't drink enough water during a game, dehydration may set in. If the body's water is reduced by 5 percent, a player may experience muscle cramps. A 7 percent loss of body water can result in dizziness and an increased heart rate.

CHAPTER 4

▷ **THE ARENA**

SOLID FOUNDATION

Most major basketball arenas have beautiful wood floors. Wood is used in indoor arenas because it is the perfect playing surface. Wood floors are constructed to have the right amount of give. A surface with more give is easier on players' feet and legs because it absorbs forces as players run and jump.

Density is often used to describe materials. Two quantities that determine density are mass and volume: *density = mass / volume*

wood

If you had pieces of wood, asphalt, and concrete that were about the same size, some would be heavier than others. The piece of wood would be the lightest because it is the least dense. Asphalt is more dense than wood, so it would feel heavier than the wood piece. The concrete block would be the heaviest because it is the densest material of the three.

asphalt

concrete

A RED-HOT GAME

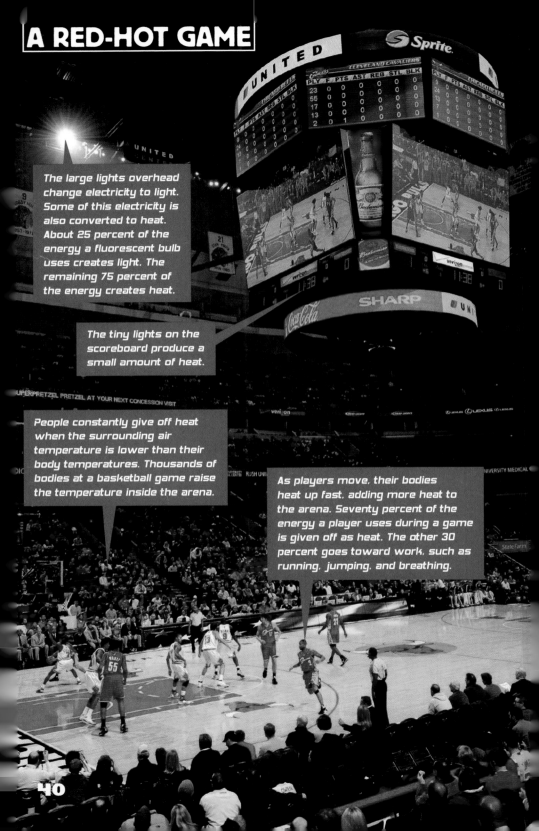

The large lights overhead change electricity to light. Some of this electricity is also converted to heat. About 25 percent of the energy a fluorescent bulb uses creates light. The remaining 75 percent of the energy creates heat.

The tiny lights on the scoreboard produce a small amount of heat.

People constantly give off heat when the surrounding air temperature is lower than their body temperatures. Thousands of bodies at a basketball game raise the temperature inside the arena.

As players move, their bodies heat up fast, adding more heat to the arena. Seventy percent of the energy a player uses during a game is given off as heat. The other 30 percent goes toward work, such as running, jumping, and breathing.

The temperature in an arena is not the same everywhere. That's because heat rises. The seats near the top are a few degrees warmer than the courtside seats. Unfortunately, those cooler courtside seats come with a higher price tag!

Basketball arenas around the country are often filled to capacity with enthusiastic fans.

The Palace of Auburn Hills in Detroit holds **22,076** fans

The United Center in Chicago holds **21,711** fans

The MCI Center in Washington holds **20,674** fans

THE ROAR OF THE CROWD

An important part of a basketball game is the distracting roar of the crowd — and thousands of people create a lot of noise. Fans cheer to pump up the players. They boo at unfair referee calls. They scream to distract the other team.

Basketball arenas are designed to focus fan noise in the stands down to the players on the floor. In a stadium with a dome roof, sounds bounce off the curved roof. The sounds then travel down to the playing floor.

Sound travels at a speed of 1,138 feet (347 meters) per second through air at room temperature.

MAKE SOME NOISE!

The loudness of a sound is measured in decibels (dB). The normal dB level in an arena during a game is about 80 dB. That's about the same dB level as an alarm clock or traffic on a busy street. But if the fans go crazy over a last-second basket, noise levels can reach more than 110 dB. That's the same decibel level as a jet plane flying overhead at 1,000 feet (304.8 meters) or a blaring rock band. Sounds at 110 dB that last for more than 30 minutes can damage the inner ear.

The speed of sound does not depend on the loudness of the sound. The sound from a fan yelling loudly travels at the same speed as a quiet cheer from another fan.

Temperature affects how fast a fan's voice travels to the court. In an arena at 65 degrees Fahrenheit (18.3 degrees Celsius), sound travels at 1,124 feet (343 meters) per second. In a 90-degree Fahrenheit (32-degree Celsius) arena, a fan's voice moves at 1,152 feet (351 meters) per second.

dB	Type of Sound
30	quiet library
50	falling rain
60	normal conversation
70	vacuum cleaner
80	normal noise at a basketball game
90	lawnmower
100	snowmobile
110	crowd cheering loudly at a basketball game
130	jackhammer
140	air raid siren

CHAPTER 5

▷ TRICKS OF THE TRADE

Fans enjoy watching basketball players with awesome dribbling and shooting skills. But cool tricks with spinning balls can also excite the crowd. A science concept called centripetal acceleration is used to explain many amazing tricks. Centripetal acceleration occurs when the object accelerates toward the center of a curved path.

▶ TRICK 1 – SPINNING BALL

The velocity of the surface of a ball spinning on the end of a finger continually changes direction. Therefore, the ball's surface has centripetal acceleration. This acceleration requires a centripetal force to push the surface in toward the center.

A spinning ball also has a different kind of momentum called angular momentum. This momentum helps the spinning ball stay upright. The angular momentum stays the same unless a twist is applied to the spinning ball.

Trick 1

THE HARLEM GLOBETROTTERS

The Harlem Globetrotters have entertained crowds around the world since their first game in 1927. Famous for their humorous stunts and amazing tricks, the Globetrotters are also a team of skilled players. They have won more than 22,500 out of 22,850 games. Through the years, new players have joined the team. These players learned the tricks from older team members.

▶ TRICK 2 – INSIDE ARM ROLL

As the ball moves in a curved path around the player's arms, three forces are involved: gravity, friction, and the normal force. The normal force keeps the ball accelerating toward the center of the curved path. Gravity is mostly cancelled by friction.

Trick 3

▶ TRICK 3 – OUTSIDE ARM/SHOULDER ROLL

Gravity and the normal force act on the ball, keeping it from falling off the player's arms. Friction keeps the ball rolling.

Exciting tricks, high-flying dunks, and amazing three-pointers — it's no wonder so many people love the game of basketball. The next time you're watching or playing basketball, think about all the ways science is a part of the game.

GLOSSARY

contract (kuhn-TRAKT) — to tighten and become smaller

density (DEHN-suh-tee) — the amount of mass in an object divided by its volume

evaporate (i-VA-puh-rayt) — to change from a liquid into a vapor or a gas

friction (FRIK-shuhn) — the force along a surface created by an object in contact with the surface

gravity (GRAV-uh-tee) — a force that pulls objects with mass together; an object has weight because the earth pulls it toward its center.

heart rate (HART RAYT) — the number of times the heart beats per minute

kinetic energy (ki-NET-ik EN-ur-jee) — a property of a moving object equal to one half its mass times its velocity squared

matter (MAT-ur) — anything that has weight and takes up space

molecule (MOL-uh-kyool) — the atoms that make up the smallest unit of a substance

momentum (moh-MEN-tuhm) — a property of a moving object equal to its mass times its velocity

revolution (rev-uh-LOO-shun) — when an object spins 360 degrees and ends in its original position

skeletal muscle (SKEL-uh-tuhl MUHSS-uhl) — muscle that is attached to bones

velocity (vuh-LOSS-uh-tee) — a measurement of both the speed and direction an object is moving

Levine, Shar, and Leslie Johnstone. *Sports Science.* New York: Sterling, 2006.

Solway, Andrew. *Sports Science.* Why Science Matters. Chicago: Heinemann Library, 2009.

Thomas, Keltie. *How Basketball Works.* Berkeley, Calif.: Maple Tree Press, 2005.

Tomecek, Stephen M. *The Science of Sports.* Experimenting with Everyday Science. New York: Chelsea House, 2010.

INTERNET SITES

FactHound offers a safe, fun way to find Internet sites related to this book. All of the sites on Facthound have been researched by our staff.

Here's all you do:

Visit *www.facthound.com*

FactHound will fetch the best sites for you!

INDEX